Enjoy!

Gary Mc

Between Seasons

More Poems
By
Gary E. McCormick

Cover and illustrations by Kathy Zerler

Other Books
By Gary E. McCormick

One of the Many Roses

Between Seasons

Published by GEM Press
Inquiries:
Gary E. McCormick
424 W. Ferry
Berrien Springs, MI 49103
E-mail: jeangarymc@aol.com

Cover and illustrations by Kathy Zerler
Printed by Batson Printing Company . Benton Harbor

ISBN 0-9630037-1-2

ACKNOWLEDGMENTS

The author gratefully acknowledges the editors and staffs of the following publications, in which some of the poems in this book, or versions of them, first appeared:

Peninsula Poets (Poetry Society of Michigan) Who *Are These Brave? Carolina Wren, A Good Sounding Word, Faith Within, Garden Colors and You, Watching God Create The Universe, From The Source, Original Sin, Explaining Colors.*

Heart Songs (Poetry Society of Michigan) Rocky *Gap Bluff.*

Poet's Review Coining *a Phrase.*

The Southwester (Southwestern Michigan College) We *Pause For This Message, Things Are Looking Up, Wind Beating Intrusion.*

CONTENTS

I.

The Power of the Moment, This Moment...

II.

My Wrinkles Seem Imperishable
As Age Scrapes Away At My Youth...

III.

Making the complex simple...

IV.

Blossoming flowers,
opening like a pure thought, sing a simple verse.

For Jean
And My Children and Grandchildren

I. Fall

The Power of the Moment,
This Moment...

Between Seasons

A thin thread of orange on the horizon
 subtly separates the seasons:
a season of falling leaves from
 a season of drifting snow,
a season of new green from
 a season of baking heat.

It is so slight this slash of color
 cutting frost from freeze,
so simple this separation
 dividing growing green from fiery red.

It's not the getting from Spring to Summer
 moving from Autumn to Winter,
it's the living between seasons that matters most.

It's this pause between seasons
 which gives our hearts time to adjust.
ours spirits cause to endure.

The Good Book

Good Hope Holiness Mission,
Boonesborough, Kentucky:
Paint peeling like the bark
Of an old rugged cross,
Tattered as the pages
Of an oft-quoted bible.
Padlocks rusted, hinges same.
For years deathly quiet
After the last holy whisper.

Close by
Princey Bell Whitlow
Nears her last breath
In hospital seclusion.

Today
She feels the strength
Of those singing Bible words
Heard when the white-washed
Mission could still hold a tune.

She looks her Maker
Straight in the eye,
Hums a powerful melody
As those glorious words
Chorus through her failing mind.

The steeple holds
an aging cross, worn but steadfast.

We Pause For This Message

My snack table trembles
 before the gluttonous tube
as headline news snippets
 show brown hollow bellies
awkwardly balanced on
 thin feeble spindles.

See the pain
 of emptiness
devour all but
 their shiny
skinbone skeleton.

See dead strength,
 eyes lethargic,
unable to chase flies.

See hunger,
 thin and craving,
sandwiched between
 thirty second spots
selling diet drinks
 chocolate bars,
lite icy beer.

Where are the tears
 in those hungry eyes?

Wind Beating Intrusion

Whirlybirds and their spinning props
Buffet the currents of calm
With their noise-awful whap-whapping.

Their wind-flapping rotors
Agitate all that's peaceful,
Slapping it into the whip of wind.

Quiet dips into its jet stream,
Slips, is smothered, then dissolves.

I think of maple seeds
Gracefully whirling into my garden.
I was young and those fragile choppers were ideas.

Another Biblical Interpretation

A new leprosy
Invades our intimate relationships.

A new compassion awakens
As the epidemic touches the roots of love:
Those deep passions of close association.

Infection spread from the original DNA,
Intrusive serpentine virus from the garden?
Freedom given, immunity removed
Another epidemic breeds untouchables.

The spontaneity of love's moment now plagued by caution.

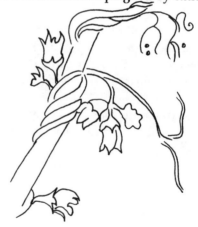

I Shot Mom and Dad

Bang! Bang! Bang!
Right between the eyes.
I still smell the nostalgia
Exploding from the roll of red caps,
As I fire away at them
Blowing up a whole winding cylinder.

Dad fakes a dead fall to the floor.
On the couch Mom slouches.
We laugh at their feigned death.

They armed me when I was five
With a pearl-handled Red Ryder
Spin-on-your-finger six shooter.

For years I fired fanciful slugs
At just about anyone who hurt me.
I mowed them down the same way
Any guns-a-blazing Hopalong would.

I think about this today as I clean my Uzi
Waiting hair trigger for society to draw on me.

Quilt

About my soul:
Its patchwork scheme
Is sewn by all those
Who touch my spirit
With the fiber of their grace,
Needles of their passion,
Varicolored threads of their love.

When I hold you close,
I'm a goose-down comforter radiating warmth.

Here Today, Gone Tomorrow

Nobody says we'll live forever,
But we sure act like we will.

Tony already makes plans
For a whole future of breathing
When he takes a direct hit
Stepping in front of a speeding taxi.

Wanda talks all day
About tomorrow and the next day,
Dreams about what life will be like
When her artery breaks and spills a bloody flood.

Jake pays in advance
Figures it will arrive in the mail.
Cancer takes another bite of his colon,
Radiation flares and slams the coffin shut.

The doctor's audacious.
He makes an appointment to get his teeth cleaned,
When the very second he scratches the time in his day planner
The earth rumbles, tumbles a whole building crashing down on him.

Cindy dreams her baby takes his first earthly step.
They feel a thousand hurricanes of air ruffle their hair,
Toss them to the heavens on ten million gusts of wind.

The writer starts the first chapter
As a bee stings him right between the eyes.
The killer closes his as he falls from the sky.

Tough Jobs

In the crush of a crowd
Clubs crack and smack
Freedom from a frightened face.

One says he's doing his job:
Smashes the skull of one
Who says you're doing
A black and blue job on me.

They're both tough jobs:
Protecting freedom
Fighting for freedom

Standing between the two
In the crush of a crowd
During a clubbing confrontation
Is another tough job.

Being a savior turned victim
Is one hell of a tough job.

What's New On The Tube

Press and networks
Reports and anecdotes
Photo ops and sound bites

Faces and numerous names
Snippets of victims, blood and bruises
Over condensed and over simplified

Kaleidoscope of pain and hope
Doomsday damned and defined
Ingratitude frame by shameful frame

New plagues of passion
Shrapnel riddled innocents
More hero and coward caskets

Everywhere on knees
People plead and people pray
Poets reach for their six-shooters

Who Are These Brave?
(In remembrance of D-Day, June 6, 1944)

Who are they?
Those who fought my battles for me.
That one, there, who fell as soon as
He touches Normandy's beach.

I see him over and over again
As the black and white D-Day memories
Repeat newsreels of chaotic heroism from all.

They keep replaying him.
Stock footage of that first one down in the surf
Killed in action for posterity again and again and again.

This invasion is a metaphor of blind courage.
Their fear and the overcoming of it spill from the barges.
And then we see him, that first one, shot dead for freedom.

Putting a New Roof Over My Head

Wind chills evict me
From the damp updraft
Of a steamy grate

Chilblains tap dance
Pins and needles
On my chattering extremes
And I go because I gotta go

Shivering I put out
My numb thumb
Turnpike down where
Palms fan the sweating sun

Under the blazing tropic dome
I suck in the ocean's salty breath
Cuddle up to a warm blanket of sand

The comfortable step over my threshold
Those threatened tell me to move on
So I set out seeking an empty bench
Singing home sweet home sweet home

Window Flags

You see them everywhere
Unfurling patriotism on windowpanes.
The Stars and Stripes say support the Storm.

Behind a bay window
A young lady watches Channel Two,
Sees her soldier boy ride his tank into the smoky desert.

Her tears burn like hot blazing oil
As she rides with him into Basra.

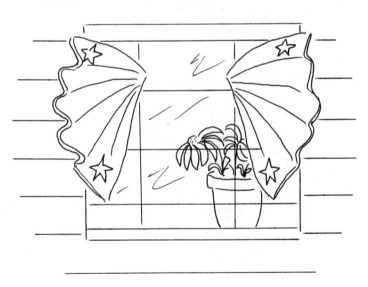

It's In The Wrapper

It's not in the running blood
Or arteries and veins
Through which it flows.

Not in the heaving heart,
Pumping it, streaming.

Surely not in the bony framework
Caging the brains and guts of life.

It's in the mask that covers the worldly
Costume of different shapes and shades.

Certainly it's our wrapper:
Subject of discriminating eyes.

Fire Fight

Just staying out of the line of fire is a chore,
As I dart in and out of every nook and cranny,
Hunting for cover while missiles whiz overhead.

Who has me cross-haired in the center of their sight?
I duck and dodge, avoiding the zip and spit of bullets,
Sidestepping whining steel, singing their ricochet.

I want to scream *stop shooting* but society keeps reloading,
Taking drive-by pot shots at me day-by-day, day in, day out.
They're still selling shooting irons, still cocking controversial hammers.

Chasers And Catchers

A white washed wave
Chases another to shore,
Catches it and sinks with it into sand.

On this stormy morning
The sun can't see beyond the nose on its face
And the sea is awash with chasers and catchers.

I'm not sure if the words will roll the way my heart implores.

Coining a Phrase

Or maybe it's
rewriting a cliché.

So my reply is to the reader
who finishes a quatrain with puzzled looks
and wrinkles on brow and brain.

I say this:
Poetry is in the sky of the beholder.

Some see whole heavens
of northern lights,
others only reflections
of flickering lamps.

And, perish the thought:
There are those who are
blind to the slightest spark.

So I take my match and strike it.

Riding Out The Tempest

Worry is a storm
 raging inside our guts.

 A woman dances away her worries
  while her man drinks his away.
Others have their own way of dealing.

Worrywarts and nervous wrecks unite:
  pray to the gods of *what if* and *what might be*.
Do it while our guts rumble and roil,
  pleading for peace in the eye of our hurricanes.

My heart eases up as I witness a blue line of dancing morning glories.

Time Out, Time In

There!

A last grain of sand
Falls to the top of the bottom
Of a feisty century's weary glass of hours.

Somewhere a second hand
Nano-skips past twelve
To initiate the clockworks of a new century.

Chimes and bells ring out then ring in;
Peal for what was, set off a new millennium's tintinnabulation.

One second a breath stops;
Then new life begins, gets going again, that very same second.

Quickly, doomsday people set their alarms;
Groggily, I shut mine off, then put two feet on the floor.

Omnipotence Enough

"To be alive is power,
Existing in itself,
Without a further function,
Omnipotence enough."
    Emily Dickinson

Sans melody
The rapper snaps
Out his loser ways of life
Like the staccato chatter
Of a runaway snare drum.

With arrogance
The slammer screams
Out a doomsday poem
Grunting expletives in
Anapestic babble.

They complicate,
Puzzle with confusion.

Emily says
It's the power
Of the moment,
This moment.

Simply,
Life's ample,
She tells us.

II. Winter

My Wrinkles Seem Imperishable
As Age Scrapes Away At My Youth...

Rocking The Porch To Sleep

My Siamese circles,
kneads and cuddles
into a ball of purr
and hums herself
singing to sleep.

My lap resonates
As I rock and doze,
buzz myself
snoring to sleep.

The nodding stars have heavy eyes.

Thirst

I'm flour dry
dusty and hoarse
with a leather tongue
gasping for a cloudburst

I dream of quenching drops
of crystal clear dew raining down
forever on my parched and withered face

I'd die for a drink.

Lone Gull, Silent Gull

A sleeping gull
Balances on one limb,
Sleeps alone on a
Long stretch of sand.

Sole spirit of shore
Escapes the swarming
Riot of cries from its
Raucous screaming family
Who fly wildly downwind.

Sleeping gull
Tell me the secret:
Does peace fly gently in the sky,
Swim softly on caps of lapping waves?
Do you find quiet tucked under your smooth wing?

Rocky Gap Bluff

The hungry lake chews the bluff
Bit by champing bit,
Spitting chunks into the wild wash.

A birch holds its ground
With skin peeled roots,
Grabbing tight with white-knuckle grip.

Boulders break loose
Scramble freewheeling,
Cartwheeling from glacial bonds.

A shooting star erodes,
Explodes across the sky.
The lake screams its reflection.

My wrinkles seem imperishable
As age scrapes away at my youth.

Explaining Colors

There are many ways to explain rainbows,
Contemplate their style of stretching stripes,
Reaching out majestically with half moon fingers.

Watch their colorful silence breaching life's clamor.
Witness the sunshine of them break down chromatically.
See wishers, wishing wishes to the glory of their powerful glow.

On life's darkest day may double rainbows
Transform your monochrome view into full color,
Light your spirit with flashes of Technicolor sparks.

There is no explaining.
Just bows of brilliant color, raining down on pots of gold.

Surround Sound

A grumbling crowd of noise
Murmurs its wild monsoon
While silence fights to survive.

And you, my love,
During the clamor of it all,
Tap painted nails
On stained oak, punctiliously.

You keep time to the hullabaloo,
Bring a semblance of tempo
To the murmuring throng:
Out of timing, out of tune.

This, I believe,
Is the metronome of your
Incessant charm:
Mute in your beauty,
Never missing a beat,
During riots of energy.

A Nest On The Ledge

All the whirling extravagances
Dance in the eye of a whipping swirl,
Whistle wildly in the fierce wind.

Frenzied squeals chant in a furious spin.
Wailing force flies uninhibited,
Bites and spits at a fragile city.

Under tons upon tons
Of steel, concrete and glass,
We sleep and ride it out
Secure in our preserve.

From the pinnacle
A peregrine sheds a feather,
Dusting the city, ever so slightly.

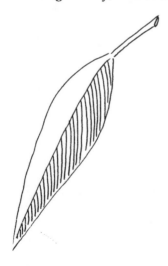

Out Of Chicago

Silent ships churn black wakes,
Wingtip reds and greens bounce
On crests of moon sparkle foam.

Sleek ships trim and tack,
Plow waves aside racing to shore
Outrunning the sinking shadows of sea.

The racing sailors are Lake Michigan riders.
They're out of Chicago bound for St. Joe,
Wishing for swift winds and billowing sails.

We know they're coming.
On the pier we stare into the darkness
Watching for the first sparks of their passage.

Mourning Rain

A storm cloud bursts
Bringing on a good cry
In the stinging rain.

Struck by calamity
Rinsed by tranquility.

Clear skies arrive as a man
Wipes tears and raindrops
From his refreshed face.

Heaven knows what tomorrow's
Weather will bring, he thinks,
Smiling through the rainy rays of sun.

Relaxing Walk

Bending a head
Swinging a foot
Kicking stones
Along a sidewalk,
Is a slow stroll
Way of walking
And unwinding.

The sun says
Slow down,
The wind whispers
Take it easy.

Me,
I'm just walking
And unwinding.

Garden Colors And You

Browsing in the garden,
  roses rouge the pink
Of your dusty face,
  violets purple the tan
Of your coffee thighs.

Watching you weed,
  daisies yellow the white
Of your sandy wrists,
  ferns green the hazel
of your blooming eyes.

Holding a bouquet
  of garden flowers,
The strawberry of your hair
  rainbows all the vivid blossoms.

Splendor
Are the garden colors and you.

From The Source

Pain?
Let me tell you about pain.

Feel the needle prick of stinging thorns
Pressed hard against the skin of my skull.
Imagine a tight crown of throbbing punctures.

Hurt?
Let me tell you about hurt.

Imagine the jeering, spittle, lash and nails.
Sense the thirst, the aching bruises.
My cry at the thrust of a sword.

Agony?
Let me tell you about agony.

Look at my mother's contorted face,
Witness the anguish of her bleeding heart.
Feel her pain, her hurt, her agony.

Evening Questions

I stroll bewildered
Asking questions
In somber shadows

Your distant light
Slightly answers
One dark question

But I have more
Heavens more

So shed your light
With a sky full
Of bright insight

Elucidate like
Exploding rockets
Brighten my sky
With your midnight sun

Carolina Wren

Shuffling on seed, like grits,
The pip-squeak flits in
From down south
Singing a high trill
Laced with a southern drawl.

Its cocky striped tail feathers
Stand straight and tall
As it struts its stuff,
Doing a rasping
Soft shoe in seed.

How can something so small
Shake the sadness from my soul?

Another Kind Of Symphony

The silver spine
  of the great lake
shivers with joy,
  excited by the music
of glorious twilight.

The composition is
  striking orange gold,
modulated with deep
  white tipped blue,
orchestrated in runs of
  sunset brilliance.

The Maestro conducts
  a sundown symphony,
harmonious in the gloaming.

I watch, I hear. I listen, I see.

A Good Sounding Word

Polly says
Chrysanthemum
Over and over again.

When
The two-year-old
Says it and sings it,
You can almost smell
The fragrance in her smile,
See the flowers in her wide eyes.

You can
Almost hear the singsong
Chime of her sublime
Chrysanthemums.

Polly's found
A good sounding word
And she likes saying it,
Singing it, over and over again.

Rendezvous

Scattered on
Lake Michigan's shore,
Clusters of spotted orange
Speckle helter-skelter
Over mottled sand
And the morning's
Flotsam and jetsam.

They're ladybugs that congregate
In crowds of dotted knots
As beachcombers tiptoe gently,
Dusting mystery with sand.

So tiny is their display of grandeur.

Things Are Looking Up

The skyscraper
Swings and bends with the wind
Giving someone a high ride
As it scrapes the sky.

Hurried crowds below
Rush by this monster in motion,
Its slight sway hidden from the throng.

A lover's bewitched heart
Rides a thermal and rises robust
As his loved one steps from a cab.

I-94 To Chicago, Near The 24 Mile Marker

Splashing through freaky January warmth
Fog becomes windshield seltzer.
A laid-back hawk fusses its feathers
In the gray skeleton of a dreary willow.

Slush puts grime in proper perspective,
As sixteen wheels bathe me in slop.
Air brakes fizz, dirty tail lights squint,
I brake left and swim through its spray,
Leave its roar in the steam of my wake.

A Mercedes passes, exposing a passenger side lady,
Whose sad eyes are as gray as the day is gray.

The Significance of Sand Glass

Lake Michigan is noisy this morning
But I take comfort in its power.

The winter storms have left the usual trash
Plus a fresh assortment of rock, stone and pebble.

How can one absorb the lake's elaborate display
And not believe in an early morning Divine Designer?

I retrieve a rare piece of sand glass
Which seems to be the broken bottom
Of some ancient bottle, sanded to a smooth feel.

It's precious to me because there's not another like it.
This makes it special and, like you, it's a rare find.

III. Spring

Making the complex simple...

Watching God Create The Universe

Making the complex simple:
Grinding rock, building beach.

Waves draw impressions:
Race, absorb, erase.
Moisture fades then hides.

Countless grains
Ride brewing bubbles.
They toss, tumble, and turn,
Shuffle ashore.

The eternal project
Continues in all its glory.

Creation continues
In the slow wash of waves,
In the harsh crash of storms.

I walk the beach and watch:
Each speck a desert,
Every drop a sea.

Faith Within

Terribly afraid I try to unearth
Some ancient sarcophagus
Buried deep in gray matter recesses.

Then some inner strength
Overcomes with a peaceful response.
Suddenly my faith within is a feather of steel.

Strength depends on tough muscle,
Courage on that rock-hard, gentle spirit.

Dad Changes Tunes
(For my father)

You must have loved us dearly,
Cared for us deeply, to trade your traps
For Ford's Rouge Steel payroll.

Henry couldn't fathom your sacrifice:
You walking off the bandstand
Into the rusty open hearth dust,
Quitting those snappy jazz solos
For its searing blast furnace heat.

It must have burnt deeply
To trade your skins and cymbals
For the fire and dust of Ford.

I think of this as I tap my foot to the
Basie beat of drummer Butch Miles.

Getting To Know You
(For my mother)

You're a depression lady,
A prohibition doll.
Free to dance, smoke and booze.

Remember our joys?
Music we shared, like the Mills Brothers'
Paper Doll lyrics and melody smiles.

We witnessed Traverse City satisfaction
Arriving at the lake and cabin
After a winding drive through the dark.
Spiritually in tune when the bay appears
Gorgeous blue through cherry orchards.

What makes me understand you more,
Now that you're gone, what makes me
Want to remember those cherished moments
Once blurred with smoke and booze,
Caught in your throat like cancer?

You loved books, loved reading, loved words.
I was transfused with some genetic romance
With words that excite, words that sing and dance,
Like Ginger and Fred dazzling together on the screen.

We wore the same hearts, cried out together,
Feeling no pain, howling for some unreachable joy.
Wounded souls sensing pain's promiscuity.

Fresh Flowers

Cherished memories
Bring splendor
To the bouquet,
Gracing the stone
Spelling your
Names in granite.

Like that rock
Your love is strong,
Its passion burning
Like the fervor
Of today's sun.

Death
Does not
Find us apart.

Little Things

Microscopes fine-tuned
  to see what the eye cannot.

Telescopes focused
  to see stars beyond the stars.

Magnifying glasses adjusted
  to examine a tiny speck.

Eyes modified
  to zoom, enlarge and clarify.

Atoms on a distant star
  hide from our sight.

From any distant star
 we are far out of sight.

Just wee bitty things are we,
  hidden from view in the
overpowering glare of starlight.

I feel so small after a whole day of being big.

That Early Taste Of Death

Wheels of a milk truck
Rolled over my best friend
One early four-year-old morning
Just a short run from my door.

Death screamed its painful doom,
Violently, in one screeching yelp.
It still rides alive and wild,
As I wait for the certain crunch
Of its resolute rolling wheels.

Original Sin

Mom said
You took
The cookie

I said
No Mom no

I survived
The lie
But the guilt
Still kills

Let it go
She cries
From some
Distant kitchen

I swear I hear
Forgiveness
Offered
Through clouds
Of eerie echoes

Family

Mother's buried downriver,
Dad in Traverse City,
Both in Michigan.

Sister's in California,
One brother in Plymouth,
Another in Canton,
Both in Michigan.

The hardest part
Of growing up is growing apart:
The folks splitting, then dying
Brothers and sisters moving
To where they're supposed to be.

They visit my mind from time to time
bringing feelings good, feelings sad:
good for knowing them, sad for missing them.

Two Blues
(For my IHM Nuns)

Blue priestess, blue tutor
  double blue habit of reverence
 vows underscored by the
  press of starchy white bonnet
blessed brow and cheeks
 shining moon tunic
background for the hanging cross
 pure milky white fingers
one holding the golden band
 of your one true spouse

You lead the young congregation
 down the aisle to altar and chalkboard
custodian with beads worn like a six shooter

Miss mysterious whose humanity
 hides in dark blue, royal blue recesses
of those bottomless pockets
 wrapped in the folds of your holy robe

I'm grateful for those early days colored by two blues

Wedding Day

In September wedding white
She thinks pleasant thoughts, dreams good dreams.

Later, with babies crying, kids screaming,
Noses bleeding, pets to pet, walls to wash,
Husband to humor, nerves to quiet from a hectic day,
She remembers those pleasant thoughts and good dreams
Wished for in September wedding white.

Now even those times are good dreams,
Remembered as she cuddles closer to her sleeping dreamer.

Diamond

Of all the rocks on earth,
The small stone you wear
Is most esteemed.

I know not
The eons of grind
That shaped
Its precious shine,
But I do know
Your finger is its throne,
And its radiance
Shows our love aglow.

If destiny commands,
I will return it with you
To regain its lasting luster.

Lonely evenings
I will look for your facets
Glistening from some eternal star.

Memories Of The Big One

The silver heads
  with wise wrinkles
talk about the invasion
  while shuffleboard pucks skid.

A scarred head with bloodshot nose
 recalls D-day and the slaughter,
tells about seeing his best friend
 disintegrate into a bloody shadow
burned in the swirls of Omaha beach.

This is a recollection of great pain
  as he hears, smells, feels that day again.
Through tears his buddy explodes out of sight again,
  as his gut feels that same nineteen-year-old nausea.

You survived the big one, somebody says,
  as their skidding disks collide.

Genesis

Metamorphosis occurs
When a Popsicle child
Powder puffs the sweet
From her cheeks and plays
Lovely lady with colored lips
And purple penciled brows.

With pluck in her green eyes
She winks at the young lady
Growing up in her fickle mirror.

Half Dozen

Are all those, yours?
Those: the two boys and four girls.
The usual question, when dining.
Eight of us with, at least, forty utensils.

Yes, answers their mother
Proud of their count and certain
Of their number as she remembers
Her joyful endurance during their birth.

Yes, thinks their father
Sometimes overwhelmed
By their number as he remembers
His awesome responsibility during their growth.

The waitress brings the menu
With offerings as varied as the individual
Makeup of each and every child,
Sharing their thoughts at today's dinner table.

A Warm Cozy Poison

You're an easy-going friend,
Only sour at first sip
Then almost velvet as you
Soothe your way down,
And lullaby me softly to sleep.

Then my spirit revolts:
Seeps into disgrace,
Bursts out my worst,
Brings on day after day
Hangovers of mind, body, soul.

I remember someone said:
Drunk took drink,
Drink took drink,
Drink took drunk.

I said: *I'll drink to that,*
Then drank myself sober.

May Our Tears Be Turned Into Dancing

You may think dear girl
That this loss is the end:
Bearing more again would
Be more than you can bear.

But I leave you my love.
Breathe deep and you can feel it.
Exhale and it won't come out of you.
It's there to stay; it's there for keeps.

It waits; it waits for that joy,
That joy of spiritual reunion
Which will come at the end of the day,
When our tears will be turned into dancing.

Sunset Revisited

The hot orange ball
Plunges into the lake
Painting the tips
Of clouds a dusty rose.

I spot a bench
Resting on the bluff
Watching the lake doze.

So I sit, behold and absorb
As the rosy glow flows
Across a sleepy sky.

Words fail to paint
A proper picture,
But I give it a try.

The Interpreter

Nature sends its messages.

The northeaster swooshes off the lake,
  sails through the leafless woods.
It cries: *there's a blizzard on our tails.*

The lake machine-washes
  a tub full of slapping waves, frothing suds stewing.
It warns: *we're awash, there's a storm brewing.*

The squirrels filibuster,
  chittering with their eerie chatter.
They stammer: *can't anyone tell us what's the matter?*

The crows squawk, squawk, squawk
  their monotone doomsday warning.
They caution: *be careful, there's trouble dawning.*

The song sparrows sing,
  making no harsh predictions.
They chirp: *there's joy coming without restrictions.*

I listen, unravel and jot it all down,
  searching for the right words.
I think: *Is it possible to explain this awe in so many words?*

Aerodynamics

A strong but pliant wall of air
Is slashed by hard wings, soft wings.

A jet sweeps and a jay swoops
Slicing angles in the atmosphere.

Hard silver wings, soft blue wings
Cut ethereal lanes in the morning sky.

Their delicate aerobatics
Move the free-falling lightness of my soul.

IV. Summer

Blossoming flowers,
opening like a pure thought,
sing a simple verse.

A Collection of Haiku

January

The Christmas tree flies
when a white blizzard barrels
into Michigan.

February

Northern birds fly in,
wind chill nipping at their tails;
cold snowy owl's numb.

March

Chilly early blooms
yearn to be summer flowers:
ivy's green envy.

Clarity

Bright inspiration;
Fresh like a crystal icing
   on this cool crisp thought.

Dear

You are so precious,
loved soul of many facets,
   my brilliant diamond.

Thaw

Ball of furnace fire
comes roaring out of hiding;
   icicles shed tears.

Inaugural

Lifting our spirits;
preserving, persevering:
    our country goes on.

Morning

The sun tips its hat.
A sparrow sings tranquility.
    Spring says *all is well.*

Mountains

The horizon grows,
beauty unfolds bit by bit;
    panoramic awe.

Poem

    Keen thoughts crowd the sky,
full heavens always unload.
      Reach up and pluck one.

Red

    Red brush from pallet,
decorate life's roses,
      color their crisp blush.

Science

    Some are so certain
it began with a big bang.
      Those who know, don't.

Spectacle

Hale-Bopp surfs the sky.
Poets write about its "wow"
    while angels gasp.

Self

Grandiosity:
standing tall yet oh so small,
    insignificant.

Tree

Wood with thin fingers,
crows rest on elbows and arms;
    laugh at each other.

Words

Your special language:
bright glowing sunset lights the
horizon ablaze.

River

Your gold ripple swims,
sparkles on toward the lake,
small splash excites it.

Quiet

Feather do your dance;
glide so gently in the sway:
hush peaceful secret.

April

Today's soaking rain
rinses the speckled snow wet.
Spring takes a deep swig.

May

Blossoms greet us:
peach, crabapple and cherry.
Awake, tasty fruit!

June

A suntan blushes.
A lady sheds her suit
for a wide-eyed sun.

Chickadee

A chipping whistle:
its happy sing-song greeting,
  a black cap's dawn song.

Lilacs

Wild color and smell
is your purple way to say:
  Spring is here right now.

Cats

Real bird lovers watch
jays smiling through the window,
  crows laughing at them.

Carousel

Carnival colored
menagerie of horses
carry children's laughs.

Civility

Leaders break the rules,
scold each other for the same
old hypocrisy.

Awe

Golden horizon
overwhelms the vast heaven:
less is so much more.

Jazz

Saxophone solos
turn melodies inside out.
Hearts start skipping beats.

Spring

Dark snow sinks below.
Fresh rebirth stirs, strength not seen.
Spring greets us with green.

Inspiration

A downer gray day,
brighter now with snow's glitter,
happy thoughts glimmer.

Spirit

Something lighter than
a feather flies toward heaven.
See its hazy wings?

Spirit Two

Putting a finger
on something invisible:
touching an angel.

Spirit Three

Amorphous body:
like a quick fleeting thought,
your powers vanish.

Intro

The beginning's loud:
booming a violent storm,
    thunder-rumbling drums.

Guardian

When you least expect
their gentle but strong embrace,
    your angels hug you.

Vapor Trails

High Chicago jets,
scribble cross-hatch in the sky.
    Angels erase them.

July

Parades, skyrockets,
flag waving day ends with a
patriotic bang.

August

It's too hot for me.
Fresh cool breeze is hard to find,
shade is on my mind.

September

Reluctant summer
slowly sashays from the scene.
A cool snap gives chase.

Lake Michigan

A quiet great lake
takes a lazy siesta
on this peaceful day.

Sun Up

Early yard's alive,
birds and squirrels do their thing.
Lax cat purrs on grass.

Rose

Red silk and soft folds
nestled on green stem of thorns.
Does the sunrise blush?

Falling Blossoms

Blossoms, oh, blossoms
falling from angel wings,
    float softly to dew.

Moon

Its full bright flood light
penetrates awful darkness
    with its eerie glow.

Drunk

Tearful bloodshot eyes,
breath of a decayed carcass;
    drink takes the lost man.

Gene Kelly

Singing in the rain.
Memories of your splash dance;
   that vamp as you leave.

Clooney

"Com'on'o my house..."
Rosie singing with an accent,
   juke box overjoyed.

Gershwins

Their words and music
bind and cherish each other,
   melodiously

Jazz Set

Jazz jumps in the crowd:
harmony, conversation,
    improvisation.

Sun

Bang! New sun begins.
A fiery sky explodes,
    its light, long lasting.

Crow

Is no nest secure,
no egg safe, from the crow's pinch?
    Warn the mothers, wren!

Cliff Swallows

The swallows dodge, dart,
flying tight close formation,
    nearly piggy back.

Music

Fill the air with song,
with melodies that sound like
    rainbows in your ears.

Nuclear

Soft plume envelops,
bright fried sun arrives ablaze,
    doleful earth shuts down.

October

The lake begins to cool.
Sails fill with a last warm wind.
Geese excite the sky.

November

The sleet won't be rain
as it tries hard to be snow.
One last leaf hangs tough.

December

Snow with colorful
reflections, trees shining bright.
All's joy in the world.

Apple

A red shiny coat
hides sweet meat from a blue jay's
quick staccato stabs.

Gray Day

Solemn is the smog,
a gathering of droplets,
heavy as a tarp.

Raindrops

Like grief tears you fall,
spotting the pink of her cheek.
Do you sob, sad cloud?

Junco

Snowbird pecks away,
shuffling seed out of the snow.
You're first to arrive.

Feeder

Wild congregation
whistles, picking goodies.
A cat licks its chops.

Lone Goose

Straggling goose struggles
as its gaggle flies away,
breaking formation

Winter

Tree of diamonds,
reflection of galaxies,
　　revealing earth's peace.

Winter Beach

White caps sculpture ice,
spray sings a cold winter song.
　　Chilled gulls catch their breath.

White Out

Whiteness blows whitest.
Wild blizzard roars, makes frosting
　　like powdered sugar.

Roof

Flakes of snow so strong
their gentleness, together,
brings down a cold roof.

Driving Snow

Horizontal snow,
smashing head on in slashes,
makes eyes close with ice.

Evening Snow

Quiet winter night,
silence falls from a dark sky.
Earth wears a white coat.

Christmas

Heaven's Special Star:
An uncomfortable birth
    safe in Mary's arms.

After Christmas

The sun cannot see
the nudity of the trees
    this December morn.

Millennium

Time again runs out.
Both sleepy feet hit the floor,
    new day, next breath.